~ *Craft Ideas for Your Home* ~

# PAINTING TEXTURED WALLS

*~Craft Ideas for Your Home~*

# PAINTING TEXTURED WALLS

**CANDIE FRANKEL**

Little, Brown and Company
Boston   New York   Toronto   London

*To Caitlin Murphy*

~

## *Acknowledgments*

*The author gratefully acknowledges the many fine photographers
and designers whose work is featured in these pages.*

~

First edition

ISBN 0-316-29141-2

Library of Congress Catalogue Card Number 94-73262

**A FRIEDMAN GROUP BOOK**

10 9 8 7 6 5 4 3 2 1

Published simultaneously in Canada by Little, Brown & Company (Canada) Limited

*CRAFT IDEAS FOR YOUR HOME: PAINTING TEXTURED WALLS*
was prepared and produced by
Michael Friedman Publishing Group
15 West 26th Street
New York, New York 10010

Editor: Elizabeth Viscott Sullivan
Art Director: Jeff Batzli
Designer: Lynne Yeamans
Photography Editor: Colleen Branigan
Production Associate: Camille Lee
Illustrator: Barbara Hennig

Color separations by Fine Arts Repro House Co., Ltd.
Printed in China by Leefung-Asco Printers Ltd.

# Contents

~

# Introduction

A fresh coat of paint has long been the easiest and most affordable way to turn a tired, drab interior into a clean, welcoming space. But even newly painted walls in exciting colors can appear flat and one-dimensional, without any intrinsic interest or depth. Today, people who want more drama in their homes are taking their painting projects one step further, incorporating centuries-old glazing and color-washing techniques into their decorating schemes. For these techniques, the wall surface is spackled, primed, and painted with a base coat in the same manner as for an ordinary painting makeover. After the walls are properly prepared, the magic begins, as one or more coats of glaze are applied to the surface. Unlike paint, glazes are translucent. Each coat of glaze that is applied allows the layers of color underneath to filter through. The result is a rich buildup of color and texture that one can actually peer into.

Highly specialized painting and glazing techniques such as marbling and woodgraining require years of practice to master, but basic textured walls can be achieved by anyone who can wield a paint roller, brushes, sponges, rags, and paint combs. The techniques are easy to grasp and offer room for experimentation and individual expression. Since every person's touch is unique, the results are as individual as your signature.

The photographs collected here are brimming with practical designer ideas that have worked their transformation on palatial and humble interiors alike. The rich colors and textures are signs of a creative, adventurous approach to decorating, rather than of great expenditure. The rest of this introduction explains how to use ordinary paint products to achieve the same masterful looks at home.

## Choosing and Using Colors

Color is truly the heart and soul of any painted wall. There are many ways to combine colors successfully, and one of the more exciting aspects of decorative painting is discovering new ways to incorporate colors into a room's overall interior design.

Most color plans start with a light or pastel base coat and then add glaze coats in darker related hues. For example, an apricot-colored base coat covered with successively darker orange- and red-tinted glazes produces a deep terra-cotta effect. The reverse combination—a lighter glaze over a dark base coat—works best if the color of the glaze is more opaque. White glaze ragged off an aqua wall several times in succession, for example, can produce a lovely summer sky look for a child's room.

Introducing a color's complement (its opposite on the color wheel) can intensify the overall palette of a wall or tone it down, depending on how the paint is applied. To give a red wall extra punch, for example, dip an old toothbrush into green paint or glaze, and run your finger across the bristles to spatter the wall at random. The resulting tiny green dots will pop out from the red background, creating a contrast that is positively electric. But the same green glaze brushed uniformly across the red surface will have exactly the opposite effect, dulling the red tones and making them softer and more muted. You can use this muting principle to advantage if you find you have misjudged a color's liveliness or overall impact on a room and want to tone down its impact without starting over.

Another aspect to consider when assembling your color palette is how adjacent rooms relate to one another. Walk through the rooms, along the halls, and up and down the stairs in your home with a critical eye, noting exactly which areas can be seen from other areas. By planning your color transitions carefully, you can ensure that each room enhances rather than competes with its neighbor. For a coordinated look, try to keep the same mood—soft, understated, bold, or bright—throughout the house, even if you use different colors to express it. Keep in mind that vivid colors look best in the bright sunlight found in subtropical and Mediterranean climates. In northern climates where the daylight is softer and winter skies are frequently overcast, extremely bright colors can look harsh and out of place.

To identify colors that reflect your personal vision for your home, take time to browse through decorating books and magazines, and make note when a room's ambience appeals to you. The wall color may be dominant in the decorating palette or it may act as a neutral background for upholstered furniture, window treatments, and accessories. Once you have identified a basic color that you think will work for you, explore its dimensions by mixing small amounts of glaze and testing them over a base coat painted on posterboard. By moving your posterboard sample around the room and viewing it at different times of day, you can get an idea of how daylight, lamplight, and candle-light will influence the color and enhance its subtleties.

## Glazes and Washes

The secret ingredient for layering on subtle texture and translucent color is glaze, a gel-like or syrupy artist's medium that can be tinted to any color and is applied over the base coat. Glaze is slightly diluted for wall painting so that you can apply it quickly and evenly in a very thin coat. Because glaze is thin and semitransparent, the layer of color underneath shows through with a soft underglow. Perhaps the most beautiful use of glazes is in Renaissance oil paintings and frescoes, where a soft blush of rose-colored glaze over the cheeks gives faces a lifelike quality.

In decorating, glaze is applied directly to a wall and manipulated while still wet to create different effects. Glaze can be dabbed off with a sponge or rag, leaving behind a textured sur-face, or it can be patterned by dragging a comb, brush, or other object across it. The concept is similar to finger painting. Once the glaze has dried, a new glaze in the same or a different color can be added and the process repeated. By varying the colors and techniques, an infinite number of uniquely textured patterns can be achieved. Developing your own methods for manipulating the glaze is part of the fun.

## Choosing a Medium

The first decision to make when painting a room is whether to use oil-based or water-based paints and glazes. Each type has advantages and disadvantages, so consider the pros and cons of each carefully, since you must use the same product base throughout the project—from base coat to final glaze—for the successive layers to bind to one another properly.

Oil-based glazes are often easier for beginners to work with, as they take longer to dry, thus lessening the pressure to work quickly. The downside of oils is that they must be thinned and cleaned with flammable, often strong-smelling solvents that must be used with caution in a properly ventilated area. Some locales have restricted the use and disposal of oil-based paint products to reduce their negative impact on the environment.

Water-based products are comparatively odorless, and wet paint can be washed off brushes and rollers with cool water. One way to "keep up" with faster-drying water-based glazes is to work in tandem with a partner, one person applying the glaze and the other ragging off, sponging, or combing. Special retarders designed to slow the drying time of acrylic paint products can also be of help.

### Oil-Based Paints
If you choose to use an oil-based system, you will need the following products:

- Eggshell or satin-finish alkyd paint
- Japan paint, artist's oils, or universal tints
- Transparent oil glaze
- Solvent (kerosene, turpentine, paint thinner)

Your base coat should be an alkyd paint with a dull eggshell or satin finish. Avoid using high-gloss or enamel finishes, which make the surface so slick that the glaze runs right off them. Purchase enough paint for one or two base coats, following the coverage estimates on the paint can. The base coat color can be ready-mixed at the paint store, or you can custom-mix your own hue by adding japan paint, artist's oils, or universal tints to white paint. You can purchase transparent oil glaze or you can make your own by combining three parts turpentine, one part double-boiled linseed oil, and a few drops of japan dryer. Like paints, transparent oil glaze can be tinted to the color of your choice. Solvent is used to thin the glaze and for cleanup.

### Latex and Water-Based Paints
If you choose a water-based system, you will need the following products:

- Semigloss latex interior house paint
- Artist's acrylics or universal tints
- Acrylic artist's medium

Your base coat should be a semigloss latex interior house paint. Avoid flat finishes when using latex paint; they are too dull and tend to absorb the glaze before you have a chance to rag it off. As with oils, the latex base coat color can be ready-mixed or you can mix your own color by adding artist's acrylics or universal tints. Water-based glaze is made from acrylic artist's medium, which is available in either liquid or gel form, can be diluted with water, and can be tinted different colors. Be sure to choose a medium that dries clear, not white.

## Preparing the Glaze

Glaze of the proper consistency glides onto walls, adheres smoothly, and, above all, doesn't run or drip. Unfortunately, there are no guaranteed formulas for diluting a glaze to the right consistency. The humidity, amount of sunlight, and exposure to air all affect a glaze's viscosity. When thinning an oil glaze or acrylic medium, be sure to add the solvent or water in small increments, as diluting a glaze is always much easier than trying to thicken it.

Coloring the glaze mixture also requires a light hand. To preserve the glaze's translucency, the color should be added sparingly; add just enough to tint the glaze without turning it opaque. Basic proportions for an oil-based glaze are six parts oil glaze, one part solvent, and up to one part color. Basic proportions for a water-based glaze are one part acrylic medium, three parts water, and up to one part color. The color can be taken from a single tube or can, or you can mix your own custom shade before adding it to the glaze.

When you are first learning how to mix glazes, mix a small amount in a disposable container (a sturdy paper cup will do) and jot down the proportions you used. Test the glaze on posterboard that has been painted with a base coat and taped to a wall to make sure the color effect is what you want and that the glaze vis-

cosity is well suited to the texturing technique you have chosen. If the glaze appears runny when you apply it or the texture you create using a rag, sponge, or comb doesn't hold up as the glaze dries, then the glaze is too thin. If the glaze is gummy and difficult to manipulate, it is too thick. When the "recipe" is right, write down the proportions so that you don't forget them, then mix a larger batch of glaze in a plastic paint bucket. Depending on the viscosity, about two quarts (1.9ℓ) of glaze should be enough to cover three hundred square feet (27 sq m) of wall surface. Always mix about twenty percent more glaze than your calculations indicate is necessary in order to avoid running out before you have completed your project. Even with a written recipe, achieving an exact color match can be tricky.

## Getting Down to Work

The comprehensive list at right covers practically every tool and piece of equipment you will need to paint textured walls, from preparing the wall surface to dry brushing a final color wash. You will find specific information about how each of these items is used in the sections that follow.

When purchasing painting equipment and tools, always buy the highest-quality products you can afford, as they will help you work more efficiently and achieve professional results. Rollers should be the spring-cage type, with ribs that support the roller pad from the inside so that it doesn't collapse. The roller pad should be thick and fluffy to hold the maximum amount of paint without dripping. Brushes should have full

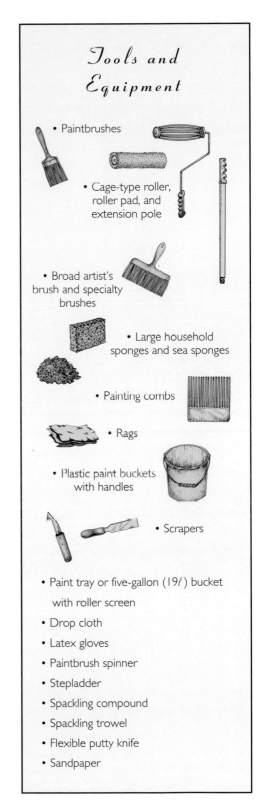

## Tools and Equipment

- Paintbrushes
- Cage-type roller, roller pad, and extension pole
- Broad artist's brush and specialty brushes
- Large household sponges and sea sponges
- Painting combs
- Rags
- Plastic paint buckets with handles
- Scrapers
- Paint tray or five-gallon (19ℓ) bucket with roller screen
- Drop cloth
- Latex gloves
- Paintbrush spinner
- Stepladder
- Spackling compound
- Spackling trowel
- Flexible putty knife
- Sandpaper

natural bristles securely attached to the ferrule (the cap that holds the bristles to the handle of the brush); when you spread the bristles apart, you shouldn't be able to see down to the wood. Sponges should be thick and absorbent. Don't overlook the importance of supplies such as drop cloths, buckets, latex gloves, and a brush spinner, for these materials will make your painting and cleanup time quicker and easier.

Finally, here are a few more tips that should help you get the job done safely and easily.

- When you open a new can of paint, take a few moments to hammer nail holes one inch (2.5cm) apart around the lip, so paint that gets into the rim will drip back into the can.
- For brushwork, pour a small amount of paint into a plastic bucket so that you don't have to carry the heavy paint can up on the stepladder with you.
- Your painting wardrobe should consist of old comfortable clothes, latex gloves, and a cap with a duckbill brim.
- Open the windows and keep the room well ventilated throughout the painting and drying periods.

## Preparing the Wall Surface

There are two approaches to preparing a wall surface for painting. One is to make sure the walls are perfectly primed, with all holes and nicks filled in and sanded smooth. This approach insures that the paint and glaze coats will adhere with a strong bond without cracking. Sometimes,

however, longevity is not an issue. You may want to simply spruce up temporary living quarters or make a room more livable while you work out plans for a more permanent renovation. If you would like to enhance a room's "character," you can patch cracks in the plaster to prevent further damage rather than completely repair them, then incorporate the cracks into a painted finish for an eye-catching "ancient ruin" effect.

To achieve a durable, long-lasting finish, you must restore your walls to the best possible condition before you paint and glaze them. This preparation phase is time-consuming and painstaking, but the smooth surface that results is worth the extra effort. Begin by moving the furniture into the center of the room, taking down pictures, mirrors, and light fixtures, and covering everything, including the floors, with drop cloths. Fabric drop cloths are recommended because they soak up stray drops of paint and give the liquid a chance to evaporate. Avoid disposable plastic drop cloths, as spilled paint simply sits on the plastic, just waiting for you to step in it and track it all over. Unscrew and remove the switch plates and outlet covers, and tape plastic sandwich bags over all the doorknobs.

Next, examine the wall surface in indirect daylight from different angles, as this is the best way to spot cracks, dents, and other imperfections. When you find a crack or hole, dislodge any loose pieces with a scraper, then whisk away the plaster dust with a soft brush (be sure to wear a particle mask). Traces of wallpaper and its adhesive can be removed using an appropriate cleaner or a steam machine. If you find any nail heads popping up, hammer them below the surface, making a shallow dent in the drywall (nails in plaster walls, if found, should be

removed). Fill in all gaps, holes, and cracks with spackling compound, using a flexible putty knife to smooth the compound over the surface as evenly as you can. When the spackle is dry, sand the surface lightly until it is perfectly smooth and even with the wall. You may have to repeat the spackling and sanding process several times, since spackle shrinks as it dries. The specific details of your wall preparation will be determined by the condition of the wall, whether it is plaster or drywall, and whether wallpaper was applied in the past.

## Priming the Walls

Once the wall surface is smooth and the dust is vacuumed away, you can begin the exciting part of your project: building the layers of color. Your first layer is a prime coat. Primer is a white paint product that evens out the blotchy tones left behind by spackling, improves the coverage of the first color coat (particularly light colors), and acts as a buffer on new, bare walls so that they don't soak up the first coat of paint like a sponge. A universal primer can be used under either an oil- or a water-based base coat and also makes a good ground when you want to apply new paint over a previously painted wall.

THE BASE COAT AFTER CUTTING IN

In some situations—for instance, if the new base coat is the same color and finish as the old one—you can safely omit the prime coat.

## Applying the Base Coat

Once the primer has dried, you can apply the base coat. To begin, brush paint into the corners and up against the ceiling, baseboard, and trims—all the areas inaccessible to the roller. This process is known as "cutting in," and for it to be effective, the paint should be applied evenly and extend a good three inches (7.5cm) from each inaccessible edge. To properly load the brush, dip the bristles into the paint until they are halfway coated, lift the handle straight up, and then slap the bristles back and forth rapidly against the inside of the bucket to shake off excess droplets. This method lets you retain the maximum amount of paint on the inner bristles, so that you can paint smooth, even strokes about two feet (61cm) long before reloading. With practice, you should be able to paint a straight edge against a molding or ceiling, but if you have difficulty, you can mask off these areas with low-stick painter's masking tape before you begin. If you omitted the overall prime coat, spot-prime the spackled areas with the base coat paint while the brush is still wet. Since dry spackle absorbs paint more readily than the surrounding wall surface, this step makes for more even roller coverage later on.

The fastest way to spread paint on the wall is with a roller. To wet the roller, fill the well of a roller tray or the bottom quarter of a five-gallon (19ℓ) bucket with paint, then dip the roller into it. To shed the excess paint, roll back and forth a few times on the tray's angled plane or

ROLLING AN M

on a roller screen hung inside the bucket. Roll a large M shape onto the wall, then spread the paint around the wall by backrolling in different directions. The long extension handle should let you reach up to the ceiling and down to the baseboard without using a stepladder or having to bend over. A second coat is optional, since the glaze coats that follow will fill in and enrich the base color.

## Creating Basic Glaze Textures

Working with a glaze on a large wall surface will be quite different from your smaller poster-board sample. To apply a glaze to a wall, work from left to right (right to left if you are left-handed) in two-foot (61cm) -wide vertical sections. Start at the top of the wall and work down, first applying the glaze and then manipulating it. Move on to the next two-foot section quickly, blending the join while the glaze is still wet. This sequence ensures that the entire surface will be uniformly colored and textured. Most glaze methods involve several steps, and you should work with a partner to keep the momentum going. One person can roll on the glaze and free-brush it, while the other can follow two sections behind to complete the ragging or combing.

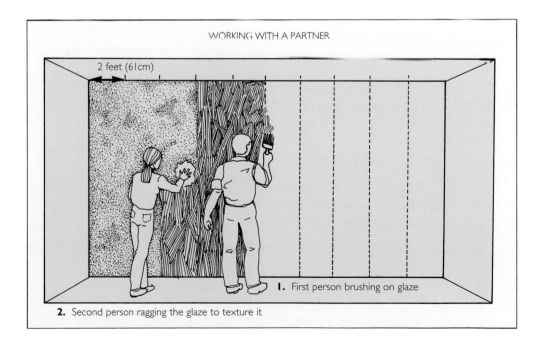

WORKING WITH A PARTNER

2 feet (61cm)

1. First person brushing on glaze

2. Second person ragging the glaze to texture it

To avoid smearing paint in the corners, paint opposing walls one day, let them dry overnight, and then complete the adjacent walls the next day. Wear disposable latex gloves whenever you work with glazes, and follow the general painting guidelines regarding ventilation. Always allow plenty of drying time between applications so that you don't muddy your previous work. Specific guidelines for ragging, color washing, sponging, and dragging follow.

## Ragging

Ragging is a general term for a variety of textured painting techniques. As the name implies, the key tool is a rag, about two feet (61cm) square. Woven linen and cotton fabrics make ideal rags, but you can also achieve novel effects with cotton knits and open-weave fabrics such as cheesecloth. The edges of the rags should be cut clean with scissors, not torn, to help prevent loose threads from escaping into the paint. Cut a generous number of rags, since you will have to replace them throughout the project as they become saturated with glaze.

You can use rags to apply diluted paint and glaze to the wall, to texture glaze already on the surface, and to lift glaze off the surface. Remember, the harder you press, the more glaze you will lift off. To apply a glaze or diluted paint with a rag, saturate the rag, ring it out well, then crumple it loosely in your gloved hand and dab at the wall surface. Another method is to form the wet rag into a tube and roll it down the wall. For a less pronounced texture, apply the glaze to the wall with a brush or roller and dab at it with a crumpled rag moistened with water or turpentine to lift the glaze off. For a two-tone marble effect, brush on the glaze in random strokes that cover about half the wall surface; rag this glaze, let it dry thoroughly, then add the second color to the open spaces and rag in the same manner. You may also wish to experiment with different ragging techniques on posterboard (see page 8) to determine effects that please you before you begin. Regardless of which ragging style you choose, the key to an interesting overall pattern is to vary your hold on the rag continuously as you dab, so that none of the impressions repeats. To avoid smears, wait until you have lifted the rag from the surface before twisting your wrist and changing the rag's position in your hand. The texture achieved with ragging ranges from

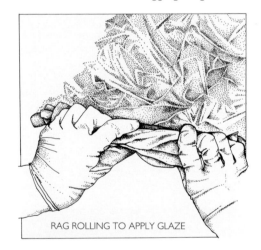

RAG ROLLING TO APPLY GLAZE

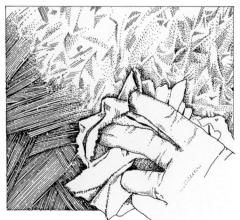

RAGGING OFF TO REMOVE GLAZE

coarse to very soft, depending on how many layers of glaze you rag and the weight of your touch. Ragging does take time; consequently some people find oil-based paints more compatible with ragging techniques than faster-drying water-based paints.

## Color Washing

Color washing is the technique to choose when you want a soft, beautiful wall finish with the fluid quality of watercolor paints. Very thin glazes are used in color washing, making it possible to build up multiple translucent layers with cloudlike depth. The glaze is applied with a roller or brush, then smoothed lightly in all directions with a sponge or a wide brush with soft bristles that leave no brushmarks. The finished surface takes on a timeworn patina that is especially effective when a hint of the base coat shows through.

Both water- and oil-based products work for color washing, although thin water-based glazes are prone to rapid drying and may not allow you enough time to smooth and blend the glaze at the edges of each application. To slow the evaporation, sponge the wall with clear water before you apply the glaze, making sure the base coat is perfectly dry first. You can also add acrylic paint retarder to the glaze to extend the drying time.

Color washes gain depth and interest when closely related colors are layered together. Terra-cotta shades are especially warm and rich, while blues appear deep and mysterious, as if you were peering into a pool of water. The subtle variations that appear from color washing can help camouflage minor imperfections or an uneven plaster wall surface.

USING A SEA
SPONGE

USING A
UTILITY
SPONGE

## Sponging

Sponging is easy and practically foolproof, making it especially attractive to beginners. Like rags, sponges can be used to apply glaze or diluted paint to a wall, to texture a layer of glaze that has already been applied, and to blot up glaze from the surface.

There are two basic ways to maneuver a sponge. One way is to dab it up and down across the surface, so that the holes and impressions in the sponge create a negative imprint on the wall. This technique is most effective with a natural sea sponge because of the odd sizes and

quirky shapes of its holes. As with a rag, be sure to rotate the sponge in your hand as you dab to avoid repeated patterns. When applying color, be sure to keep moving the sponge around. Don't linger too long in any one area or you will lose the detail and totally obliterate the background color.

The other method of sponging is to wipe the edge of the sponge lightly across the surface in short random strokes that resemble brushwork. If you lift the sponge slightly as you complete each stroke, you can create a lovely feathered effect that is especially effective when second and third colors are added. A large utility sponge works best for this technique.

If you are sponging off and the sponge becomes too paint-logged to continue, wring it out before proceeding. For smoother manipulation of glazes, moisten the sponge first. Water-based paints are preferred for sponging, but oil-based paints are workable, too. If you are concerned about water-based paints evaporating too quickly, sponge the wall with clear water before applying the glaze.

## Dragging

Dragging produces the most pronounced texture and pattern of the four techniques discussed here. The glaze is always applied to the wall first, and then a comb is pulled or dragged through it in a straight line or with an undulating motion to create a pattern. You can buy special painting combs with long teeth at art supply stores, or you can cut your own versions from coffee can lids or other stiff, smooth plastic. Brushes with stiff or short bristles are also suitable for dragging and can be used to produce wood-grain effects.

Dragging requires patience and precision. You must drag the comb or brush in a smooth continuous motion without any jerky stops or starts to mar the pattern. When you start a new "drag," you must move the comb directly alongside the previous drag to equalize the spacing and camouflage the join. Even movement and seamless joins are difficult to achieve on long ceiling-to-floor stretches that require climbing up and down on a stepladder. You may prefer to limit your first dragging effort to a more easily accessible area, such as the dado beneath a chair rail. Another option is to drag in short intersecting spurts, for crosshatching or basket-weave patterns that resemble coarsely woven fabric.

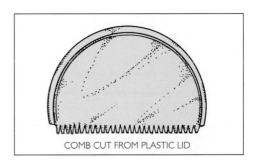

COMB CUT FROM PLASTIC LID

13

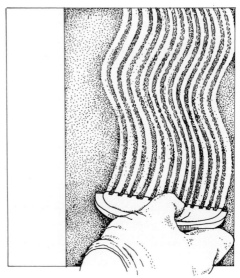

COMBING IN A WAVE PATTERN

# Cleaning Up

Painting a room is a big job, and the end-of-the-day cleanup can seem monumental if you don't approach it systematically. Water- and oil-based paints have different cleaning requirements, but each method will benefit by the use of a paintbrush spinner. This ingenious gadget, sold at paint and hardware stores, works like a child's hand-pumped spinning top to rotate a freshly cleaned wet brush or roller at a very high speed until it is almost dry. (Be sure to point the spinner down inside a deep bucket when you spin to contain the spray.)

To clean water-based paints, act promptly before the paint has a chance to harden. Rinse messy brushes and rollers under cool running water until all traces of paint are gone. Liquid dishwashing detergent can help loosen the paint and make it glide off more readily. Spin to remove the excess moisture, reshape the brush bristles as necessary, and lay the damp brushes or rollers on a table or counter edge to dry. If the paint or glaze is particularly heavy or gloppy, rinsing and spinning several times in succession may be necessary. Plastic buckets can be rinsed clean in cool water.

Oil-based paints require a two-step cleanup process. First, you must use a solvent, such as turpentine or paint thinner, to break up and dissolve the paint, and then you must use sudsy water to wash away the solvent. Work in a well-ventilated area, and wear latex gloves to protect your hands. To clean a brush, pour a small amount of solvent into a clean plastic paint bucket, and recap the original container. Dip the brush bristles into the solvent (holding the bucket at an angle to pool the solvent), then

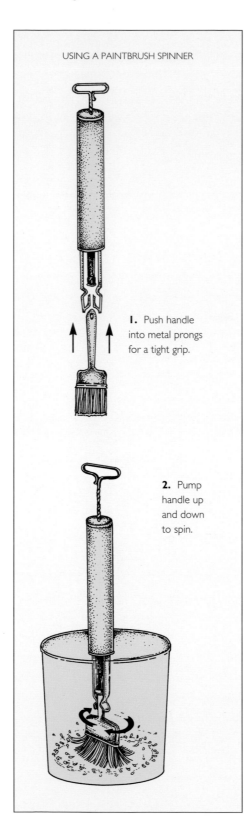

USING A PAINTBRUSH SPINNER

**1.** Push handle into metal prongs for a tight grip.

**2.** Pump handle up and down to spin.

press the bristles against the inside wall of the bucket to release the pigment.

To clean oil-based paint from a roller, pour solvent into a flat pan with sides and set the roller in it, turning the roller to moisten the entire surface. The solvent will absorb only so much pigment, so if the brush or roller is particularly saturated, you may need to repeat this step several times with clear solvent to remove all the residue. To speed the cleaning, spin between the dippings. Follow up with a sudsy wash and a final spin. Damp brushes and rollers can then be left to dry as described in the paragraph on water-based paint cleanup. Buckets and tools can be cleaned by wiping with a rag dipped in solvent, then washed with soapy water and dried.

For economical and environmental reasons, used solvent should be recycled rather than poured down the drain. Pour the solvent into a clean glass jar, screw the cover on tightly, and set the jar in an out-of-the-way place where it won't be disturbed. In a week or two, the pigment will settle to the bottom, leaving behind clear solvent that can be reused.

In the photographs that follow, you will see the textured painting techniques of ragging, color washing, sponging, and dragging brought to life. Included are glazed walls that simulate ancient stone ruins, luminous colors that seem to glow from within, and rooms that use a combination of techniques to achieve exquisite faux finishes. The depth of color and beauty that can be achieved with ordinary paint products is astonishing and far exceeds the range of flat paint-chip colors available to decorators. How far you take the techniques is part skill and part imagination in your desire to make your home a special place.

# Reviving the Past

## WHEN NEW LOOKS OLD

Taking comfort in the past can be a great pleasure. Old furniture, textiles, pictures, and books have a humbling influence, serving as cultural reminders that our contemporary perspective is but one way of looking at the world. Those who truly cultivate their love of old things throw the impulse to update and modernize into reverse, striving instead to make the new look old, and the old look older.

Using freshly applied paints and glazes is an affordable way to give even a modest home the personality, character, and lineage of time-worn surfaces. Nondescript walls, floors, and furniture can be believably transformed into faux stone, sunbaked adobe, terrazzo, marble, and other textures that have historical, cultural, or regional associations. The resulting decor is satisfying to live with, as it approaches the room in its entirety instead of focusing on the furnishings alone.

The "new" old finish is practical in yet another way as well. A real stone wall is cold and damp, real marble loses its polished sheen over time, and century-old plaster eventually chips and disintegrates into powdery dust. The faux antique finish, in contrast, requires practically no upkeep and, with the application of a proper sealer coat, can even be washable.

This section features a variety of distressed surfaces that were actually created in recent times with contemporary paint products. Each surface achieves a sense of age and permanence that enhances and lends dignity to the decor.

~

*Opposite:* Aristocratic homes and furnishings that show signs of benign neglect convey an aura of romanticism. Here, one or two layers of a lightly tinted green glaze allow a hint of natural wood grain to show through, suggesting a paint finish that has been wearing away slowly for a century or two.

~

*Left:* A plaster wall, with its intrinsically rough surface, made a convincing canvas for a faux stone façade. To suggest venerable age, contrasting highlights were applied at random with a rag and deliberately kept simple, subtle, and few in number. The opening of the beehive fireplace, in contrast, was surrounded by a broad band of slate blue paint in order to magnify its unusual shape.

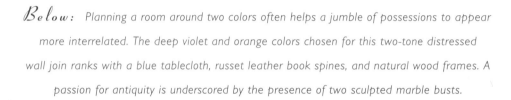

*Right:* A spattered paint finish above the chair rail and warm yellow tones below it spark some life into a grand room gone to seed. The small fortune needed to restore such a home often comes in fits and spurts, making a quick yet inspiring intermediary decor a necessary option but providing the chance to test future color combinations in their actual setting.

*Below:* Planning a room around two colors often helps a jumble of possessions to appear more interrelated. The deep violet and orange colors chosen for this two-tone distressed wall join ranks with a blue tablecloth, russet leather book spines, and natural wood frames. A passion for antiquity is underscored by the presence of two sculpted marble busts.

18

*Opposite:* The plain cement floor of this entry hall gained instant patina when terrazzo stripes were painted on its surface. The glaze bears realistic scratches and scuffs, a clever artifice suggesting the foot traffic of a busy nineteenth-century hotel lobby. Placing the floor stripes and a marble-topped table on the diagonal helped to cordon off two corner doors that are no longer in use.

*Below:* To draw out the warm glow from the hearth into the room, the walls, fireplace, and ceiling of an adobe-style home are all treated with the same apricot wash. The subtle color variations that emerge when the wash is applied help soften and camouflage irregularities in the plaster surface. The finished surface creates a magical backdrop for dancing evening shadows.

*Above:* A gently ragged wall makes a restful, understated backdrop for antique fixtures, such as this three-armed brass sconce. The dull patina of the brass would look dirty and unpolished against a crisp white wall, but here it glows softly against a salmon glaze's hand-rubbed blush. Note how the dark red and brown glazes emphasize the vertical molding at the left.

*Opposite:* The soaring ceiling that infuses a home with precious light and volume rarely offers personality as well. To rescue this contemporary living room from all-white sterility, the fireplace wall was washed with a dull, brick red glaze and then distressed using a variety of techniques. The finished wall stands like an ancient ruin in the middle of the room, as if the rest of the house had been built around it.

~

*Below:* Paint is often used instead of stain to camouflage different types of wood that appear in the same piece of furniture or construction. In this upper-story alcove, the look of an architectural built-in was achieved with stock moldings, ordinary drywall, and a simple unfinished wood desk. To unify the various elements, a succession of glazes ranging from emerald green to deep turquoise was brushed on each surface and then ragged off. The muted, gently striated patina that resulted looks decades old.

~

*Above:* When a collection of tailored furnishings starts looking too rigid and premeditated, a softly textured wall may be all that's necessary to tone down the hard edges. Everything in this room exhibited crisp, geometric lines, from the marble-topped bureau with gold-banded drawers to the sleek, satin-covered chesterfield chair. The ragged wall introduces an unimposing feminine presence that shows off all the pieces to advantage.

~

*Left:* A fresh coat of paint followed by selective light sanding turned a bank of ordinary twentieth-century kitchen cabinets into an oversize colonial dresser. An antique with original paint that might flake or peel off has no place in a food preparation area, but this deliberately distressed finish, which can be duplicated on new unfinished wood furniture as well, makes an impressive substitute.

23

~

~

*Right:* A charming built-in
bookcase was a seldom
used and basically overlooked
amenity when the walls of
this entry foyer were painted
the predictable white. A
fresh color washing with yellow
glaze brought the framed
unit back into focus and
inspired a cozy correspondence
corner, complete with a
dog bed. Other pieces were
added to complement the
new romantic mood, among
them the landscape painting
propped casually at the
back of the desk.

24

~

*Below:* An effort to strip away stubborn layers of paint left behind a mottled surface with lots of tactile interest. To soften and integrate the remaining fragments, a light, neutral glaze was washed over the entire wall. Like a building that has stood the ravages of time, the resulting finish imparts solidity and permanence. A chair studded with bottle-caps in a tramp-art style stands in sharp contrast and adds a contemporary touch.

*Above:* To give this old-fashioned utilitarian bathroom an air of luxury, the remodeling budget was sunk into a custom-made pink marble tub surround. The walls were ragged in a deliberately subdued gray to avoid overpowering the marble's delicate pink veining. A salvaged overmantel with a mirror mounted above the tub adds a quirky touch and prevents the all-white fixtures from appearing too clinical.

25

26

~

*Above:* A bedroom in a subtropical climate feels a few degrees cooler when the walls are painted to
resemble large blocks of gray stone. The gently mottled surface is neutral and unobtrusive, underscoring
the room's serene monotone furnishings and classic white louvered shutters. Adjusting the movable shutters
to deflect the light also helps to cool the room.

~

*Left:* A few hairline cracks wandering across the surface of a plaster wall make a sympathetic accent to a piece of antique needlework mounted for display. The golden ecru color washing matches the needlework's yellowed fabric, bringing the exquisite green embroidery into relief. Additional green tones appear in the trio of pillows grouped on the settee below.

~

~

# *Living Color*

## ROOMS THAT GLOW

Color is never static. Its mood changes throughout the day, responding mercurially to passing rays of sunshine, heavy clouds, and lamps that glow in the evening. The intensity and natural beauty of any hue is greatly enhanced when glazes are used to build color on a wall or floor surface. Color is, after all, reflected light. When there are more layers to reflect, the color is enriched without necessarily turning darker or losing its initial sparkle. Adding those multiple layers requires patience, but the results are worth the effort—and watching the color develop and intensify is pure pleasure.

The photographs in this section capture the variety of color moods that glazes can bestow upon an interior. Some of the rooms have muted watercolor hues that are soft and cloudlike, while others exhibit strong tactile properties produced by ragging and combing techniques. Whatever its mood, each setting is a trailblazer, opening up new color territory on the home frontier.

*Opposite:* A lush golden wash spills from the ceiling onto the walls of a dining room, suggesting a luxurious private chamber in a marble palace. The creation of enclosed, elegant interiors is an art practiced by restaurateurs who want to provide their patrons with a brief escape into another world. The same sense of privacy, security, and pampering is always welcome at home.

~

*Left:* Ornate architectural moldings in Victorian homes were traditionally gilded and painted in several colors to highlight the details. Unfortunately, century-old wood, gesso, and plaster moldings are prone to chips and dents, and shrinkage can cause entire sections to break off. Here, a deep green combed glaze brings out all the beauty of an old decorative molding while camouflaging its imperfections.

The power of color in interior design can not be underestimated, for color is perhaps the most basic and pervasive influence a decor can impose. One color will draw people into thought, and another color will draw them out of themselves. Chosen wisely, the colors in a home will cheer, uplift, and invigorate the occupants as well as relax, soothe, and pamper them.

*Below:* To give an oval mahogany partner's desk a contemporary air, its complement, a deep teal blue, was chosen for the wall finish. The softly ragged wall has a cloudlike quality that offers an especially restful vista after a period of concentrated reading or paperwork. The blue lampshade reinforces the serene scheme, while leafy palm fronds add lushness to the view.

*Above:* A tight floor plan allotted only the bare minimum of space at the foot of this L-shaped staircase. To help regulate the traffic flow, a side wall was glazed a sunny yellow, and a rectangular, knotted rug was laid on the floor. Those descending the staircase have an easy glimpse of both the wall and the rug, allowing them to navigate the passage with greater ease.

*Left:* Yellow walls would have appeared too playful and unsophisticated for this essentially spartan interior, hence the solution to go half and half. The yellow dado adds sunny color without overwhelming the space with frivolity, while the white wall above makes a fitting backdrop for a traditional religious print. The overall result is contemporary and elegant in its simplicity.

31

*Right:* Both natural and artificial light spread their individual auras across this bedroom wall, demonstrating the range of intensity and tone that a single paint color can hold. In bright daylight this coral wash appears pale, but in evening by lamplight it takes on a warm orange glow. Both tones complement the blue striped bedspread and painted bedstead, cabinet, and chair.

32

~

*Below:* Reversing the usual color assignments can give a room a mysterious, surrealistic air. Unlike typical interiors, in which walls are lighter than floors, this dining room features a dark mahogany wash above a pale ecru carpet. While visually out of the ordinary, the juxtaposition is also serene, perhaps due to the room's minimal style and the warmth of the wood furniture and moldings.

33

~

*Above:* A stepped half-wall—part of a larger cutout entry—created a sweeping vista between the living room and dining room in this home, making color coordination between the two areas essential. To avoid the monotony of a single color, the dining room walls were glazed, then brushed on the diagonal to create a textured effect that looks windswept. The contiguous vista is harmonious, yet each room retains its own identity.

*Below:* In rooms used primarily for evening entertaining, rich dark walls create a romantic, seductive aura. The evolution of this wall's color scheme—from apple green to dark green to ultramarine to midnight blue—arouses more interest than jet black, yet is no less sophisticated. Against the wall's deep colors, a seating arrangement in cinnamon and orange hues stands out like a sparkling jewel.

*Above:* When the architectural details of a room are as grand as this, nothing else should steal center stage. To help the walls recede into the background, a deep peacock blue glaze that matches the chair upholstery was washed over them. Gold-toned marbleizing on a white ground, in turn, focuses attention on the fluted pilasters, deep baseboard, and decorative cornice molding. An Austrian shade echoes the dappled colors and freestyle motion of the veining.

*Left:* A wash that intensifies the closer it gets to the ceiling imitates nature's sky, which always appears lighter and less saturated near the horizon. Framing the imaginary vista are decoratively painted leafy arches, which, along with the mini-étagerè/ and uniquely shaped light fixture, imbue this small, rather utilitarian bathroom with Old World elegance.

35

*Left:* To make a wide entrance and sweeping square footage appear even more spacious, the walls were colored with sky blue glaze. The cool color visually recedes, making the far wall appear farther back than it actually is. Dark brown diamonds stenciled onto the floor suggest a distant vanishing point and provide a strong contrast to the sky effect. Despite the preponderance of blue on the walls and furnishings, a small addition of white woodwork, red throw pillows, and eclectic wall sconces dressed with black stars keeps the mood vibrant and upbeat.

*Above:* Placing "earth" colors below and "sky" colors above proved to be a successful formula for painting a main-floor entry foyer. Each surface—terra-cotta walls and the light blue ceiling—is framed by pristine white woodwork to distinguish it from the other.

38

~

~

*Below:* To give the intrinsic beauty of free-form and symmetrical patterns an opportunity to stand out, try placing them side by side. This glazed wall was dragged with a comb from various directions, creating random contours similar to those seen in aerial photographs of cultivated fields. The symmetrical patterns on the adjacent drapery panel appear all the more precise in contrast. The secret to the juxtaposition's success is that the two walls are similar in tone.

~

*Above:* Drawing attention away from a high ceiling is essential to creating intimacy in a cavernous bedroom. On the far wall, a chalky blue glaze lends a hand by extending no farther than the standard height of ceilings in newly built homes. A lineup of small framed photos on the mantel and a bust on the hearth also help draw interest downward, away from the formal ancestral portrait looming above.

~

*Left:* This unusual architectural space featured so many interesting angles, ledges, and built-ins that there was no obvious focal point. To provide some contrast, a deep cornflower blue glaze was washed across the fireplace wall. Inspired by the terrazzo kitchen floor in the foreground, the blue glaze complements and thus sets off the golden-toned wood furniture and floor.

39
~

~

*Right:* Standard bookcase units can provide welcome storage, but if they don't fit the wall space, they can look gangly and have no real affiliation with the room. To consolidate these matching units along one wall, fluted pilasters were placed between them. Stock molding closed the gap between the shelves and the ceiling, and also doubled as pediments. To ensure that the pilasters stood out, the surrounding walls, ceiling, and trim were glazed and ragged in soft green and dusty pink tones that provide unity and color yet fade softly into the background.

40
~

~

*Above:* A sense of intimacy was hard to create in this high-ceilinged room, partly because the towering windows kept diverting attention up from the seating area. To emphasize the lower half of the room, an orange-red dado was ragged all around. A large red bolster cleverly extends this line straight across the window seat, while the other furnishings were deliberately selected to fall below the new chair line. Above it, the ragging texture continues to create warmth but in hues that are less intense, thus providing a sense of space.

~

*Opposite:* Red is the stereotypical color choice for bistros and family restaurants, for it is known to stimulate the appetite and arouse the taste buds. In this dining room, almost everything is colored red, from the ragged walls and massive corner cupboard to the patterned tablecloth. The saturation enables the few remaining pieces to stand out in startling contrast. Note how the white ceiling provides visual relief from all the excitement without taking away from the drama.

~

*Below:* In a formal home, the vestibule conveys the tone and style of the overall decor. This generous entryway welcomes visitors with warmth and a sense of order, yet the apricot color-washed walls hint that there might be some fun surprises in the rooms beyond.

43
~

~

*Above:* Displayed against a white wall, a beautiful collection of blue and white chinaware platters simply faded into the background. To provide more contrast and show off the shapes of the platters better, the wall was washed with a pale tangerine glaze, another example of how opposites on the color wheel can create strong visual interest.

44

~

*Above:* Paint that simulates expensive stone makes for a rich juxtaposition of colors and textures. In this postmodern tableau, a brilliant turquoise surface, ragged to imitate malachite ore, sharpens the steely edge of the industrial shelving. The wall and shelving work together to show off the vulnerable beauty of two long-stemmed tulips in a crystal bud vase.

*Left:* Striped fabric and a boldly combed wall surface are natural companions, no matter what the decor. In this formal setting, romantic balloon shades sewn from yellow tone-on-tone striped fabric mimic the soft vertical striations on the adjacent wall. More stripes appear on the gold-edged lamp shade. For the best overall ensemble, the various groups of stripes should be of different widths and different but harmonious shades of color, rather than exact matches.

45

~

*Opposite:* Three tiers of color are a fine way to break up the monotony—or the intensity—of a single-color room. This design places a heathery field at eye level, a sunny yellow band around the upper perimeter, and a tropical turquoise sky overhead. The blue of the ceiling works to open what might otherwise be a cramped space, and the transition from heather to yellow creates the same horizontal line as an old-fashioned picture-hanging molding. The pale aqua dots added to the mauve surface prevent the ceiling from appearing aloof.

~

*Above:* Small rooms are the perfect canvases for trying out bold decorative strokes that can be overpowering elsewhere. In this bathroom, black paint applied to the wall with the edge of a sponge mimics experimental acid etching. A seamless mirror extends the image like a Rorschach inkblot, blurring it ever so slightly in a watery haze. The entire scheme is futuristic yet has an Art Deco feeling, thanks to its chrome fixtures and sleek black surfaces.

*O*pposite:  With windows on three sides, this enclosed porch made sleeping here almost like camping under the stars. To enhance the room's outdoors feeling, an olive green wash was lavished on the side wall, and turquoise paint was applied to the top and bottom of the window frames to open the room to the sky. The striped Hudson Bay blanket on the bed turns the alcove into a bona fide bunkhouse.

*A*bove:  Abundant natural light streams through a glazed door and a skylight—thoughtful amenities for a dark interior vestibule and stairwell. To further blur the distinction between outdoors and in, the walls were washed with a peach glaze and crazed with a rag to resemble sunbaked adobe. The stairwell is framed with wide, rough boards that are usually reserved for exteriors and outbuildings.

Right: *Taking its color cues from nature, a built-in breakfast nook places a darker ocean blue closer to ground level and a lighter sky blue above it. A mustard gold chair rail fills in as a sunny horizon line accented by witty punctuation marks. The light blue wall pales considerably in the lamplight, but the wash is actually quite evenly applied. The soothing colors provide a tranquil backdrop for the eclectic mask and hubcap collection.*

*Above:*  Bright, lively paints cheer up one end of a narrow efficiency kitchen that could easily feel

claustrophobic. The banana-colored walls look sunny even on overcast days, and turquoise paint makes twins

out of two mismatched chairs. The red-topped cabinet doubles as a table for quick meals and snacks.

~

*Opposite:* Choosing a trim color that is similar, rather than contrasting, can help establish either a cool or warm color scheme. Here, a brilliant turquoise wall is accented by a deep powder blue trim, which creates a cool color scheme and suggests a tropical sea and sky. Other pieces in the room—a rosewood display cabinet, a black upholstered tub chair, and a chrome lamp with a white-frosted shade—are cool in hue, too.

~

*Above:* Choosing accessories first is a sensible approach to decorating classic black and white–tiled bathrooms, which look fabulous no matter what colors are used as accents. This wall palette is a sophisticated take on the multicolor-checked shower curtain. The classic water jug print inspired the marbled effect, created here by sponge-wiping. Keeping all the colors the same tone ensured that the finish would be subtle, despite the range of colors used.

Seeing a wall as a blank canvas means looking beyond customary decorating solutions to new possibilities. Many homes are overly dependent on white walls, those silent partners that show off paintings, sculptures, and collected objects with museumlike objectivity. While stunning in a public space, the "gallery" look offers a private home little warmth or uniqueness.

One answer to white-wall rigor mortis is a colorful, decorative wall finish. Moving the locus of color and texture away from objects and onto the walls represents a major shift in emphasis that immediately bestows a room with personality and presence. No longer simply a shelter for a treasured collection, the space becomes a cherished treasure itself.

The exciting faux landscapes, marbled walls, and architectural niches on the pages that follow demonstrate how any ordinary flat wall can figure more prominently in the decor. Some of the wall treatments here fully transform the space by adding new vistas or dimensions, while others contribute in more modest ways. By coordinating existing furnishings with the finishes—or sometimes eliminating the furniture altogether—daring new rooms are created for not much more cost than that of the paints.

Classic or offbeat, playful or somber, decorative finishes painted today show a generous spirit. They are a precious sign of creativity, invention, and individuality. Single-handedly, they can inspire even the most mundane interiors to come alive.

*Left: Everything in this comfortably furnished bedroom revolves around a deep mahogany hue, which surfaces in the carpet, dressing table, textured wall, and bedspread. The magnificent serpentine spines on the dressing table give the room a quirky charm, with their unique, surreal presence cleverly underplayed by the matching wall treatment, a compromising solution for roommates with divergent tastes.*

*Below:* Corinthian columns flanking a templelike display niche appear all the more dramatic when the adjacent walls are painted to resemble stone. The depth of the niche gives the impression that the stone is several feet thick, promoting a sense of solidity and sanctuary. The only giveaway is the painted switch plate near the molding at the left.

*Above:* Walls that are plain architecturally needn't lack geometric interest. Each zigzagging band on this dining room wall is glazed in a different color, accentuating the momentum of the design. Using tints and shades of the chosen palette ensures that no color is repeated yet helps all the colors remain interrelated. The suedelike texture was achieved by ragging off the wet glaze with a wad of cheesecloth.

*Left:* Generously sized doors that open onto a pass-through from the kitchen made this dining area ceiling seem disproportionately high. To foreshorten the walls, a chair rail was added around the room, dividing the wall into two sections. The dado was colored with a dark russet glaze so that it would appear as an extension of the floor, while the remaining wall above was painted in a lighter tone and thus reads as the "real" wall. Each section is textured with the base coat color of the other, a clever way to draw the two sections together.

57

*Right:* When a room's natural vista is less than attractive, a gifted hand can paint a scene to suit one's fancy. This beautifully rendered landscape turns an ordinary dining room into a balcony overlooking Tuscany's hills. Continuing the sky on the ceiling fosters the illusion of endless open air, while the columns at the front of the picture plane unify the mural and the architecture of the room.

~

*Below:* Here, an unusual paint finish spills from the wall onto the floor. A monotone texture can appear especially surreal in a windowless entry or hallway when there is little in the way of furniture or other visual clues to communicate which end is up; in this case, a tapered-leg console table lends a helping hand.

59

~

~

*Above:* Unfortunately, the gaping black hole of a heating vent was on permanent display in this otherwise light and airy foyer. To draw attention away from the vent, a textured painting technique resembling tiger's maple was worked on the lower wall, while the grating was painted white to help keep the eye focused on the triangular grillwork rather than the blackness looming beyond it. A console table placed above the vent helps to conceal it from the casual viewer, too.

~

*Below:* A collage of architectural prints, decoupaged directly onto the wall, called for a unique underlying background. The apt solution was a ragged surface that resembles parchment. The prints were affixed to the surface, and trompe l'oeil rings, cords, tassels, and frames were added last, completing the artful deception.

~

*Above:* Envisioning a niche and statue where neither exists is a first step toward transforming a flat wall into one with pictorial depth. A professional artist used various ragging, washing, and brushwork techniques to produce the trompe l'oeil effect shown here. Far from playing second fiddle to the real thing, a rendering such as this possesses a life and spirit all its own.

*Left:* Marbleizing all four walls would have over-whelmed this compact dining room, so just one surface was decorated. The paints used for the mustard walls and olive-glazed bookcases were repeated in the marble veining for a highly coordinated look. Slightly darker shades in the veining echo the bronze mirror frame above the chair.

61

~

*Opposite:* The fixtures of this compact powder room were awkwardly placed, giving prime floor space to an inaccessible corner. To minimize the flaw, a pleasant mural draws the eye up and out beyond a trompe l'oeil trellis to a cloud-filled sky. The bas relief, trellis, stone half-wall, and birds are all hand-painted on the wall surface with perceptive detail.

~

*Below:* When painted details play a supporting role to other furnishings, a convincing stage set can emerge. Here, a past-its-prime couch was draped with a red throw and kilim rugs, turning a dull corner into a vibrant mideastern bazaar. Lending credence to the transformation is the wall's low dado, painted with a series of Moorish-inspired ogees.

~

*Above:* A built-in bank of cupboards and drawers provided much-needed storage for audio and video equipment, but the wood's light tones proved too informal for the room's decor. A conservative dark green glaze helped the cabinets gain a little majesty and recede gracefully into the background. The individual panels on the cabinet doors were ragged to show off the moldings that surround them.

~

*Below:* In a room used mainly at night, dark, mysterious colors are appropriately seductive. The swirling tortoiseshell pattern on the wall was created with rags and brushes, offering a labyrinth of visual delight no matter when it is viewed. The interest intensifies at night, when the dark colors seem to envelop and protect the room. Deep red drapes that draw shut complete the enclosure.

~

*Above:* An allover ragged texture in a light color enhances, rather than interrupts, the strong, solid lines of a gabled ceiling. The mottled ecru texture resembles parchment, a fitting choice for this masculine retreat with continental furnishings. A printed wallpaper border edges the skylight above adds a feeling of space.

*Left:* When accessories are bold and strong-boned, a background that extends rather than saps their energy is a must. Here, wavy combing creates an invigorating backdrop for a Venetian mirrored sconce, a moody landscape in a silver frame, and an Italian side chair: all three pieces have sinuous curves that are echoed in the combing. The effect is dynamic, even though the glaze is a subdued taupe.

*Right:* A section-by-section analysis reveals the secret of a fireplace mantel's charm: it is actually a glorious assemblage of stock lumberyard moldings. Each piece is meticulously hand-painted to resemble quarried stone in real and fanciful colors. The quirky look is amplified by the ocher paint chosen for the wall.

66

~

*Below:* Here is a vase of flowers that never needs replacing. This vestibule was too narrow for a console that could hold a vase of real flowers, so the wall was updated with a trompe l'oeil vase in its own Romanesque niche. Architectural moldings and a broken pediment above the doorway inspired the classical theme.

~

*Above:* In an attic room, a combination of horizontal and vertical lines helps to minimize the wall's strong upward slope. Both architectural and painted details appear in this classical, symmetrical decor, and each is so perfectly executed that only close inspection can distinguish the faux from the real. The sunny yellow and white palette is particularly suited to a setting where dormered windows compromise incoming light.

~

*Above:* When strong geometric lines dominate a room's landscape, playful colors can help lighten the atmosphere and make architectural details appear less rigid. In this bedroom, aqua, yellow, and gold glazes color the panels, molding, doors, and wall so that they appear less serious and imposing. Upon completion of the project, the all-white ceiling looked conspicuously bare, so it was washed with an aqua glaze and given its own mock panel, too. Note how emphasizing the rectangular and square shapes points up the marbleized foot of the bed.

~

*Below:* Any surface in the house is fair game for painted design. This rug design makes sense under the window, where it can be appreciated, instead of on the unsealed floor, where it would have been worn away by foot traffic. Note how the paint colors pick up the yellow ceiling and red door.

~

*Left:* Accomplished and budding artists alike can appreciate the informal canvas a pair of old kitchen cabinet doors provides. If a painting effort doesn't pan out, the doors can always be painted over or replaced. This abstract harlequin design, rendered in mirror image, was a definite artistic success.

69

~

# Sources

~

All of the necessary tools, equipment, and paint for textured wall projects can be purchased at hardware and paint stores, or larger discount stores with hardware and paint departments. Some of the smaller specialty supplies, such as acrylic medium, sea sponges, and japan paints, are available at art supply stores. Once you begin painting textured walls, you will become aware of different tools and how they can be of use to you. But always buy the basics first—a quality brush and roller, plastic buckets, and a stepladder are essential to working efficiently—and add the extras as you need them.

One way to learn more about painting textured surfaces is to take classes. By studying under an experienced artist, you can gain valuable insights into more challenging techniques, see actual samples of finished surfaces, and develop your skills under the watchful eye of an expert who can shepherd your progress. Classes are conducted in a variety of settings: adult continuing-education programs, adult summer craft camps (vacation packages that let you immerse in week-long craft classes in a relaxed setting), museum-sponsored one-day workshops, and, for the truly serious, artisan certificate programs and apprenticeships. To find out more about these opportunities, consult local newspapers, college bulletins, and the classified advertisements and calendar listings in craft and decorating magazines. Your local public librarian can be a tremendous resource in helping you make the contacts you need, too.

# Further Reading

~

Drucker, Mindy, and Pierre Finkelstein. *Recipes for Surfaces: Decorative Paint Finishes Made Simple.* New York: Simon & Schuster, 1990.

Hemming, Charles. *Paint Finishes.* Secaucus, N.J.: Quill/Chartwell Books, Inc., 1985.

Innes, Jocasta. *Decorating with Paint.* New York: Harmony Books, 1986.

———. *The New Paint Magic.* New York: Pantheon Books, 1992.

Spencer, Stuart. *Marbling: How-To Techniques.* New York: Harmony Books, 1989.

## Conversion Chart for Common Measurements

~

The following chart lists the approximate metric equivalents of inch measurements up to 20", rounded for practical use. To calculate equivalents not listed, multiply the number of inches by 2.54cm. To convert 36", for example, multiply 36 times 2.54, for an equivalent of 91.44cm, or 91.5cm when rounded.

| | |
|---|---|
| 1/2" = 1.3cm | |
| 1" = 2.5cm | 11" = 28cm |
| 2" = 5cm | 12" = 30.5cm |
| 3" = 7.5cm | 13" = 33cm |
| 4" = 10cm | 14" = 35.5cm |
| 5" = 12.5cm | 15" = 38cm |
| 6" = 15cm | 16" = 40.5cm |
| 7" = 18cm | 17" = 43cm |
| 8" = 20.5cm | 18" = 45.5cm |
| 9" = 23cm | 19" = 48cm |
| 10" = 25.5cm | 20" = 51cm |

# Index

# Photography Credits

© Grey Crawford: 21 (right); 30
    (right); 32; 33 (left); 35; 51; 54;
    68 (right)
© Tria Giovan: 2; 16; 17; 18 (both); 22
    (right); 33 (right); 38 (left); 40; 41;
    52; 61
© Kari Haavisto: 57; 59 (right)
© Mick Hales: 45

© images/Dennis Krukowski: 6; 15; 19;
    22 (left); 29; 30 (left); 34 (left);
    36; 38 (right); 43 (both); 59 (left);
    60 (both); 62; 63 (right); 67
    (both)
© Richard Mandelkorn: 47; 56 (both)
© Bill Rothschild: 24; 64 (left)

© Tim Street-Porter: 20; 21 (left);
    23; 25 (both); 26; 27; 28; 31;
    34 (right); 37; 39; 42; 44; 46;
    48; 49; 50; 53; 55; 58; 63 (left);
    64 (right); 66; 68 (left); 69

Drawings: © Barbara Hennig, 1995